Is It a Baby Animal?

by Bridget Taylor

Designer: Sacha McCoskrie

Credits: cover t ©istockphoto.com/Eric Faulknor, cl ©shutterstock/Tony Campbell, cr ©istockphoto.com/Eric Isselée, b ©istockphoto.com/Eric Isselée; **1** ©shutterstock/Tony Campbell; **2** ©Photolibrary; **3** ©istockphoto.com/kycstudio; **4** ©GK Hart/Vikki Hart/Getty Images; **5** ©Daniel Cox/Photolibrary/Getty Images; **6** ©John E Marriott/All Canada Photos/Getty Images; **7** ©istockphoto.com/Eric Gevaert; **8** ©istockphoto.com/Geoff Whiting

Copyright © 2010 by Scholastic Inc.
All rights reserved. Published by Scholastic Inc.
Printed in the U.S.A.

ISBN-13: 978-0-545-26643-7
ISBN-10: 0-545-26643-2
SCHOLASTIC and associated logos and designs are trademarks
and/or registered trademarks of Scholastic Inc.

5 6 7 8 9 10   08   19 18 17 16 15 14 13

SCHOLASTIC INC.

New York Toronto London Auckland Sydney New Delhi Hong Kong

Is a kitten a baby animal?

A kitten is a baby cat.

Is a puppy a baby animal?

Yes it is.

A puppy is a baby dog.

Is a cub a baby animal?

Yes it is.

A cub is a baby bear.

Is a duckling a baby animal?

Yes it is.

A duckling is a baby duck.